Praise for

A Little Book of Extraordinary Love by an Ordinary Person

"With this book, Denise smashes convention and tells the reader just how easy it is to bring love into your life, by living it yourself! This little book packs a very large message, and is virtually guaranteed to attract the reader into loving situations, in places that nobody would have guessed! This message totally transcends religion and dogma to help show us how we can be best in our essential nature: totally loving human beings. Denise gently reminds us of the most important lesson we are all here for: that in the end, everything can be reduced to love."
-Andrew Lutts, Author, *Manifesting Magnificence*

"In this rare gem of a presentation, Denise Carey shares a pragmatic and useful roadmap that can help anyone realize their true potential through love. Blending powerful universal insights with fun, practical ideas and activities, each page unfolds an extraordinary awareness that encourages us to experience and express our innate unconditional love for profound and lasting change in ourselves and our world."
-Harold W. Becker, Author and Founder of The Love Foundation
www.thelovefoundation.com

"Denise Carey has written a lovely, inspired and inspiring book on love. Her genuine heart shines through every page, and the joy and optimism she expresses are contagious. This quick read will uplift you and remind you of the power you possess to make the world a better place...and her simple, beautiful ideas will give you hope and make you smile."
-Steve Taubman, Author, *UnHypnosis*
www.stevetaubman.com or www.unhyponsis,com

"This little book is an easy read with a profound effect. Guaranteed to uplift your spirit and add joy to your life!"
- Noah St. John, Author of *The Book of Afformations*® and Founder of Power Habits® Academy www.NoahStJohn.com

Acknowledgements

In chronological order: With gratitude and joy I thank my Mother, who started me on my path into matters of spirit. I want to honor Father Doyle at Camden Catholic High School, who taught me that "there is no evil, all there is in the world is love and the absence of love." Much love and thanks to the most wonderful husband in the world who lives his wisdom and love so naturally. I adore you.

Gratitude to John Orr, my meditation teacher. I want to thank Wayne Teres for giving me opportunities of a lifetime to expand myself and for 10 years of telling me to "breathe."

I want to thank the Direct Selling Women's Alliance, an organization empowering the direct sellers of the world, for connecting me with incredible men and women who taught and believed we are all powerful beings. You can find them at: www.dswa.org.

Loving thanks to Lisa Wheeler Knight, who taught me that rewrites can be fun and humorous. I need to say that my heart and happiness in the last years belong to Dana Phillips, who freed me from thinking that accomplishing things had to be filled with worry and dread and to balance my life with joy and celebration.

I want to thank all of my Facebook friends for posting all of their positive and uplifting thoughts that got me through my own gray days.

This book would never have happened without Andy Grant, who pushed me into believing that we all have a sacred mission to be creative and to share our greatness. You can find him at: http://navitascoach.com. Also a huge thank you to

Lee Stone and his Mind Food CD, for opening me up to listen to my higher self. You can find him at www.leestone.net. And thanks to Tony Geron for being magical! www.energyhealingbytony.com

I want to thank the people who read my first drafts and helped me stay the course with their wisdom and encouraging words: Jennifer Carey, Ric Connover, Steve Taubman, Dana Phillips, Andy Lutts, Harold Becker, Krishna Raj, Pam Myrick, Margaret Harrell, and Elvena Lutton. And of course, my husband.

I cannot possibly list all the authors and positive influences who made a difference in my life, since I have been reading related materials for self-growth for about 50 years. But I must thank: Andy Lutts, Jack Canfield, Noah St. John, Steve Taubman, Eckhart Tolle, Deepak Chopra, Marcia Weider, James Redfield, The Buddha, Neale David Walsch, Esther Hicks, Ernest Holmes, Jane Roberts, Panache Desai and Daben and Orin, and Chris Cade.

Much thanks to my kind and patient editor, who stuck it out working with a new writer with questionable computer skills. My deepest gratitude to Kate Hannisian and Blue Pencil Consulting. And more thanks to Jeni Miller, my own personal tech support department.

And because it is important to practice what you preach, I want to thank my own self, for granting me the permission to boldly express my dream for a more loving world.

Table of Contents

A Note from the Author: Why I Wrote this Book   7

A Little Introduction- - Why Love?   9

Chapter One: Love Starts with YOU!   12

Chapter Two: Out and About Love   18

Chapter Three: Social Media Love   22

Chapter Four: Target Love   28

Chapter Five: Weather Love   32

Chapter Six: "P.A.P." Love   35

Chapter Seven: Walking Love   42

Chapter Eight: Action Love   44

Chapter Nine: Gratitude Love   48

Chapter Ten: Food Love   53

Chapter Eleven: Time Travel Love   56

Chapter Twelve: Breathing Love   63

Time to Celebrate!   68

You Take Over from Here   71

A Final Word   71

A Little Something Extra   72

A Note from the Author: Why I Wrote This Book

Dear Reader,

This little book is pretty informal, and "light-ish" in tone. The very fact that you were drawn to read it is thrilling to think about. You see, we are already connected in some delightful way. Let us begin our reading relationship together to add more love to all we do. All we need to do is switch our inner dialogue to one of joyful appreciation. This little book will help you do so and in turn affect all people, places and things you ever come in contact with. That seems a tall order for such a small book for sure, but you will see, dear reader, you will see.

Before you continue, please know that in truth, I do not feel that I really "wrote" this book. It just poured out of me. I've tried to keep it as honest to that "pouring" as I could. So just pretend it is 3:00 a.m. and we are sitting around the kitchen table in a sweet conversation. Add an inner smile and a deep awareness that your inner wisdom brought you to this message of love. After all, you could be reading something else, right?

They say you should write about what you need to learn. So here I am, well into my sixties, just learning about and trying to live in "agape," the Greek term for universal love. The Buddhists have a term for it, too: "metta," or loving kindness for all sentient beings. There are all kinds of ways to be loving and it is my intent to help you find, see, remember and live love in your everyday life.

We will both learn more about *being* love in every moment that we possibly can. Along the way we will have some fun, make discoveries and create a better inner and outer world for all of our planet. Mostly, we will remember that we are each a loving being ourselves. In this remembering, together we will find our way to love ourselves even more. And as Harold Becker says: *"Ever expanding love inspires an ever evolving reality."*

As a way of paying it forward, I will donate a portion of the profits from this book to charity. It is a book about love, after all...thank you in advance for sharing your love with others.

May your days be filled with love and joy, and remember this book was written with great love for you. Let's have some loving fun!

Yours in grateful love,

Denise Carey

A Little Introduction: Why Love?

"Love dispels fear, the more you love the more fear disappears." – Osho

Why does it matter that we become (or remember that we are) beings of love? In truth, it is a matter of survival. That's all. You see, until we deeply understand that *love* is the true survival instinct, and not fear, we are doomed to repeat the mistakes of the past. I am really an optimist to my bone marrow and I believe that every drop in the ocean matters. If we all put a few drops in the ocean every day it would rise. We all can change our path and move away from a fear-based mind-set to one of deep and abiding love, and this begins within each one of us. If each of us is one of those drops, our drops of love will create larger ripples that will turn into waves that soon will become a tsunami of love. If we see the power of NOT being loving to each other making the world worse than paradise, then simple logic would say that adding more love will also have an influence. We see the negative results of hatred and fear so clearly, yet we do not acknowledge that we can counteract this? You have the power! We have that power!

Terri Van Horn says: *"Small acts, when multiplied by millions, can transform the world."*

You have the power to make a significant contribution. In fact, *we all* have that power, simply by becoming that constant drop of love in the ocean for yourself and for me...for everybody.

You may use this little book in many ways and at any time, in any way you choose. Open it at random when you feel the need, read it though and just let it rest within you, or every day practice one of the love tips. You may even choose to practice one or a few for a month at a time until they become a part of you, and then practice several others. Of course, you can devise your own pattern. Everything is good, since your journey is perfect for you. Because your journey is so special, I have added spots in this book for *you* to come up with ways to create your own individualized "drops" in the ocean. Think of this book as just the beginning and as starter suggestions. Trust your inner GPS to guide you forward.

I do want to add that the *IMAGINE* sections are very important too. My hope, as more and more people read this little book, is that we all take the time to imagine the world as a more loving place. As we ALL do this, we will be making a vibrational change in our future. Thoughts are things, they lead to actions, so please gift yourself a few moments to really engage your imagination in seeing the world as a more loving place. Imagine what would happen if we all did?

Know that this book is a kind of paying it forward for me. I have gone through "the dark night of the soul" myself and the reason I am here at all is because of the accumulated help of many who have gone before me. At age fifty I was suicidal, but thanks to all of my readings and spiritual explorations I, happily, noticed that my "outside" reality had not changed, but it was only my inner thoughts that had. Bam! It hit me that I "could" be helped, and that my severe depression must be a chemical imbalance. I would never have gotten to this point had I not been a student of self-help. How lucky that my inner path has been based on the wisdom of so many, both dead and alive. Here and there in the book and in the acknowledgement section, I have thanked many of them. But you see, the smile of a child and the bright night sky are also worthy of a "thank you." So, as you read, please know that this little book is not from "me" at all, but from all that I have lived and witnessed. If you find one tiny opening to more love for yourself and the world around you, then all who have helped me get this little book to you will have been honored.

Please look at reading this book as joyful play, mindful expansion, fun feelings and a way of being of service to yourself and the universe! Since I feel this book is being written through me, and I have no idea *who* is writing this book, I just want to say thank you so much! Whatever this magical force is, I offer to It much love and appreciation. The process has been so much fun! Read on!

Chapter One: Love Starts with YOU!

"You have been criticizing yourself for years and it hasn't worked. Try approving of yourself and see what happens."

Louise Hay

Since feeling love comes from you, it really needs to start with you. I know, I know, this can be a tricky thing. Real self-worth is not in our American mind-set, as illustrated by a story about Mother Teresa's visit to a large city here. As she walked down the busy street, she was struck by the desolation and sadness she saw on the faces of the people racing by her. She was very saddened and she said working with people in poverty in her own country seemed a much easier task than trying to cure what she saw in our faces. She can feed and clothe them, but there was not much she could do for us. She saw the anguish in our souls. Even the Dalai Lama was struck by our inner sadness and personal discomfort. Someone explained that we suffer from low self-esteem. That term was not a condition he understood, so it had to be explained to him.

We all can use a little self-love. I don't mean pride or ego; I mean that genuine understanding of our personal self-worth and uniqueness. That feeling of inner strength that does not depend on looks or wealth, you know, that part of us that the economy or advertising and marketing have no control over. True self-love that does not depend on anybody else's approval. So we have to begin by loving ourselves before we can even think we can love another. Otherwise we are just using the people we *think* we love, to cover up our own black hole of fear. This is obviously not where we want to come from, right?

"Don't be hard on yourself, there are plenty of people willing to do that for you.

Love yourself and be proud of everything you do. Even mistakes mean you're trying."

Susan Gale

lessonslearnedinlife.com

Joyful Love Tip #1

So love starts with you. This first practice may seem to be a very strange thing to do if you never have tried it, but eventually it does get easier! When you look into the mirror, send those eyes love. Even if you cannot feel it, say: *"I love you!"* Part of you knows you are whole and perfect, that part that you came into this world with, before those who were less skillful filled you with fears, lies, and their misguided knowledge. The *real* you, that precious baby filled with unconditional loving spirit, is still deep within. Think of him/her when you say this…that pure spirit just new and fresh…and loving. Yep…that is the *real* you! *I love you!* Cuddle that baby, hug that baby, feel the warmth of that baby who just was not given all the love he or she needed. Love starts with you. *Remember* that you are still that inner child that longs for the loving you may have missed. Good news! You can supply your vulnerable self all that you need. I admit it may feel odd and that it may take time, but it is well worth the effort. Here is a start to filling in the blanks you may have missed.

Look into your eyes and say "I love you." Or "I am a wonderful person" or "Gosh I'm great." Maybe say: "I am a loving person," or "I am doing and being the best I can be." Pick a loving phrase that rings true for you.

Imagine the world filled with loving and secure people who are all trying to love themselves. Here is where you can really begin to change the world, your world. If you can love yourself just a *little* more, your entire relationship with your surroundings will morph into better relationships, more action and positivity. The *how* you see everything will alter. Life will be better.

One way to start is with our inner dialogue. And we all have that inner critic. A bully voice if you will. Negative self-talk is just a bully that you developed to protect you from allowing that higher, more sensitive, gentle part to show. Society has caused us all to lie to ourselves and to be defensive. Our real strength is to *be* our real truth, and that truth is *love*. I double-dare you to begin to silence the voice of that negative bully. Begin by lowering the volume of that voice. Then each time you look in the mirror and see your loving self or you hear the bully, simply say, "Thanks, I do not need you now" and smile, either inwardly or outwardly, whichever works at the time. *This simple awareness of hearing your critical voice and thanking it and releasing it will change your life.*

Believe it or not, you *can* thank your *bully voice*. That voice that tells you that you are unworthy. That voice that feeds you negativity and fills you with insecurity by making you feel *lesser than,* you can send it love each time you notice it. Soon you will no longer be needing its services. Oh, be sure that it will find sneaky ways to stay; however, your growing self–love can and will conquer all! (Keep in mind that this voice was needed to protect you in the days of lions and tigers and bears, and now is really only needed to keep you from walking down dark alleys at night.)

We all have the responsibility to leave this world a better place than we found it, so simply by loving yourself more, you can and will make your world better. Imagine if we all did this! That is why it is important that we all learn how to emanate more love. We *are* that drop in the ocean! And in fact, we *are* the ocean!

LISTEN: Hear that voice in your head? Not the bully but the one that responds to the bully. It is the voice that never changes and keeps *you,* the REAL <u>you</u> present. This voice is a sign you have a higher version of yourself, too! By the way, listening to that softer and lasting inner voice will be a recurring theme in this book. Am I saying that you have two voices in your head? Yes, the voice that is observing you and very quietly, whispering even, and kind of watching what the bully voice (ego) is saying. This is the eternal you. Think of this voice as your first inner awareness. Now, think back to your earliest memory. That pure awareness is the real you. If you can stay closer to this softer original voice you will feel less "bullied" by your inner critic. Original self-love will nurture this new loving you, the real you. You see, this original awareness has been told it was, bad, stupid, fat, and lesser than since we were born. Think of it, the most important thing in the delivery room was your first cry, and since then well-meaning parents tried all they could to stop you from crying. Everybody waits for your first word, then you are told to be quiet the rest of your school life. Makes you wonder, right?

Playful Practice: Love Starts With You

List a few ways that you can send loving thoughts to yourself. The ideas you come up with will stick, you see, only you know when this unkind voice appears most often.

Here are a few starters:

Look through your day and pick three times or places where you will try to remember to give yourself some love.

Examples:

1. Looking in the mirror when washing your hands

2. When you hear your name, or "Mommy" or "Daddy"

3. Dressing in the morning

Some more suggestions: If you have a work badge with your picture on it, look at it every time you use it and send yourself love. Do the same when you see your driver's license or other photos around the house. Oh, and when you are taking those selfies, send some love to yourself.

IMAGINE: What if every baby were given the unconditional love she or he needed? (Of course, that would mean perfect parenting from people who also had this gift bestowed on them, but we are imagining so reality has no place here.) Spend a few seconds imagining this world of perfect love… No crime, no wars, no pain, and probably very little "dis-ease."

Your Turn: Grab a piece of paper and list other ways you can build your love for yourself. In truth, this is the most important gift you can bestow on yourself and the world. Listing ways to build self- love gives us more love to share.

Chapter Two: Out and About Love

It is amazing what you can make happen when you are out of the house going about your day. Any place that has a large mish-mash of humanity will do. An airport, a mall, a college campus? You choose. While you're out and about, instead of saying nasty things in your head or thinking the people you see are pitiful, simply send every person you look at some pure, non-judgmental unconditional love! You can do this any way at all that feels good for you. Just keep it pure, no adding "if only" or "I wonder if." In fact, no inner dialogue of any kind, like "this person must be stupid" or on welfare or a terrible parent, etc. No back stories please, because such negative comments also come from that bully voice trying to inflate your ego by bringing others down.

When I send out love, I pretend my eyes are sending out beams of sparkling love and I shower them with glitter. People look up and smile! Really! Then you can make eye contact…and Yowza! You are connecting. It is so delightful. You will love being out and about doing errands, waiting in line or shopping!

Next, send love to *everything*! We know everything is made of energy and science has proven we can make protons move by thinking about them. You will want to check out *Playing the Quantum Field* by Brenda Anderson. So send loving "energy" to everything while you are out. Send it to the cars on the road, their drivers, the houses you pass and their inhabitants, trees, and animals. Be outrageous and send it to absolutely everything! I did say *everything*…even the things and people you do not like, the things and people that are unpleasant, the things and people that hurt you. Send love to anything you see or read or come in contact with.

Next, use your ears and send love to sounds all the sounds you hear and then the *big* one...get ready for it.....send love to everything you touch.

My mother was magical with her touch. Even as a child I saw how she handled things, how she performed every task with grace and care. She was a registered nurse and even in her seventies, when she worked the night shift in a nursing home, she was the only person who could get some patients to eat. I know it was because of her loving touch.

Basically, you can become a generator of love, by:

> Sending it through your eyes,

> Sending it to everything you hear, and

> Passing it from your heart into your hands.

There is a beautiful prayer by Saint Francis that starts with these words:

"Make me an instrument of your peace. Where there is hatred let me sow love.....where there is darkness light..."

I have included this prayer at the end of the book. Even if you do not believe in anything other than your loving nature (which is all we really need to do anyway), you may enjoy the beauty of this prayer. Its essence is that we can all become a total instrument of love in all we do, in every way, all day.

If you do this, soon you will feel like an enlightened being. And you will begin to act like one too! You'll feel like you know a big secret, and you will get out of your head and out into the world, in the worst situations. Shhhhh…do not tell anybody this, but your entire view of life may change. As you project love, guess what happens? It comes back to you! Just watch for it.

Joyful Love Tip #2:

Become a Love Generator: Send love out -- send it to every person, place and thing, to every thing or person you see or hear or touch! Remember this includes pets and all animals, yes, even spiders and snakes, should you see them.

LISTEN:

To your softer voice in your head, thinking of the kinder, gentler world. That is the voice of the loving being you really are.

Playful Practice: Out and About Love

List crowded places that you will frequent in your travels this week where you can practice "out and about loving." Try to pick places you may visit as part of your weekly routine. Some other examples may be: when you go for coffee, when you are at the movies, or anytime you are in line or even walking down the street.

IMAGINE:

Take a moment to imagine what would happen if everybody did this in the entire world? See all these people sending love out to their personal experiences as they go about their day! What if everybody were taught to do this as children? How would the world be? Think of it! Schools? Businesses? Your job? Your family? What a wonderful world it would be indeed!

Chapter Three: Social Media Love

We have a most powerful tool to use in spreading love: social media!

If you were attracted to this book, then you are already on the positive side of love. You see, you are wanting more love, seeking more love and aiming to have more love…so you will! When you are using social media, I am sure you get a bit uncomfortable with the non-loving messages. Maybe even some of the funny messages leave you not wanting to re-post them. I also am sure that you are already attracting other like-hearted people and messages. Perhaps you are downloading uplifting images and have friended people whose posts you are aligned with. Celebrate any or all of this. It is the law of attraction at its best and *you* have the power to increase the positivity of the Internet and therefore increase *love*!

Remember, we are aiming to love without an agenda, to spread love, non-judgmental love for all, no matter their religious beliefs. I am not asking you to be untrue to your belief system but to remember that humankind comes in many forms, shapes, sizes, spiritual and political beliefs. If you are negatively impacted by something, you may indeed reply, but wait until you can say it without heat. Remember, we are all trying our best and no matter what another person believes, that is their path toward love and joy. They are not living their beliefs just to please us.

Offering openhearted responses from the "biggest-picture" perspective that you can see is best. That voice in your head should not come from a "convincing" place, but rather from a desire to simply help another person see an alternate way to view something. Thank them for the opportunity they have given you to add to the conversation. Ask them to think about "what if." For example, "what if" all people followed their way of thinking? What would the world be like in another generation? Most non-loving thinking is short-sighted and self-serving. So gently offer an alternative. We need not fight for peace and love. That oxymoron has killed millions for centuries. We simply need to *be* and *show* peace and love to all beings we encounter.

Social media is a *huge* "blessing" because it is so powerful. (I do not use the word blessing often because it can be loaded with religious overtones.) You can choose to share only good, loving posts with no violent language or images. Yes, there are many funny, sarcastic posts that have a nasty bite. Sarcasm can be a hoot. I admit I can have a twisted sense of humor, too. But spreading things that show or promote nasty, classless behavior serves no one. If we want to use social media as a higher good, we can promote an upper-case mind-set, simply make raising our loving awareness as our goal. Together we can share millions of loving thoughts.

Be sure your Facebook page (or any other social media platform that's now popular) is a reflection of the higher "you" that you want to be. Your messages are adding to the drops in that ocean. Send out more goodness to others with the intention of spreading more joy and love, and you will get more in return.

Here's another little tip, since we are sending love with every touch, send love through your fingertips when typing your social media posts. Remember to send love through your eyes to what and who you see online. Just set the intention when you power up your electronic devices.

Here is a *huge* way to share the love when you are gaming online! When you see those thousands of people playing your game, simply send them a heartfelt inner shout-out of love! Are you asking for a "life"? Send love. Are you sharing your scores? Send love!

Remember, what you post goes round and round and is passed along and followed, too. You may even see it again yourself if it gets reposted someplace or by someone else. With the reach of social media, you have the power to create more love than ever.

Joyful Love Tip #3:

Use all social media platforms as instruments of loving kindness. When you use your computer or smartphone, know you are helping all you contact to have a better day. Use this powerful source to be your expansion of love. (Even your passwords can reflect this, so every day and every time you log in, you are reminded you are a loving being.) Social media is in its infancy, let us all become part of its *loving* foundation.

LISTEN:

Listen to that voice in your head *before* you start to type something Feel your body -- what added "heat" are you feeling? If you feel tension, anger, or disgust, *stop* and send love to yourself. Send love to **that** voice, because it is the voice in the habit of fighting back. Remember, you are not being attacked by a tiger. Send that love to yourself and maybe back away and reply later *after* you have put your thought into more loving terms. We cannot change the world until we change ourselves, and Love will do it.

Playful Practice: Social Media Love

Take a moment to review how you spend your time connecting with others by using social media or online gaming. Remember texting and phone calls rock as a way to send love too! Each time you reach for an electronic device or turn one on, you can send love. Most of us have some sort of schedule or pattern for when we check our computers, phones or tablets. So bring awareness to your social media use. Track how much time you spend each day using an electronic device and thrill yourself with the notion that you can send so much love to others

IMAGINE:

What would Facebook or Twitter or the next hot new communication medium look like if everybody used them to send loving thoughts and uplifting information? What a massive mind change we could have worldwide! Think of what *you* can do to put more love into cyberspace? What if even just *your* followers and friends would do the same? Wow! How about those gamers? You have great power in your hands! Really, imagine it now! Social media tuned into LOVE media, whooo hooo!

Loving Reminders Page

Joyful Love Tip #1: Love Starts with You

When you look into the mirror, send those eyes a loving positive message.

Joyful Love Tip #2: Out and About Love

Send love to everyone and everything you see, hear and touch while you go about your day.

Joyful Love Tip #3: Social Media Love

Use social media to add love to everything you post, even sending love through your typing and texting fingers.

Please allow yourself to remember these tips and the rest in this book in a light, joyful way. Don't worry if you don't practice all of them every day, because anything is better than nothing! This is not supposed to be hard or a "have to do." This is just a collection of loving suggestions from another soul (me) wanting to make the world a gentler place. No worries, because all drops in the ocean count! We are all the ocean, so thank you! Thank you! And thank you again, for even imagining a better world! Imagine if we all did! (Guess what my favorite song is? Yep, "Imagine" by John Lennon!)

I have a Facebook page just for you so you can share how you have chosen to add love to all you do.

Please join in on the fun with other readers and help us all add more love to our world. Go to **Just Add Some Love** on Facebook and add yours!

Chapter Four: Target Love

I say "target" love because it is like you are going to play Cupid for yourself and aim an instant arrow of love to wherever and whenever you need it.

This is really cool! I double-dog dare you to try it! Ready? Here we go…

Send love to *your* emotional states! *Whaaaaat?* Yep. Anytime you are in a negative state of mind, you really are in need of self-love. You see, your not-so-kind reactive state is the signal. Let's say you're out in your car and you flip off another driver, either for real or in your head. Send a loving thought to yourself. Why? Because *you* need it, silly. That driver is not responsible for your reaction, you are! So send your momentary, unskillful reaction a loving thought. When we react in a harsh way, we actually make ourselves the <u>victim</u> of another person's behavior. We start a nasty story in our head about how *they* are bad people. We even assign them not-so-polite names (not to be mentioned here). We label their mental capacities and add ugly personality traits, all in an instant, right? But in truth, we have no idea why they cut us off. Maybe they really just did not see us. (I know I have done that.) Maybe they are rushing to the death bed of a loved one. Yes, in fact, they may simply actually be all those nasty things we just screamed at them. But what a poor little pea brain we turn into because of something that really is of little significance, except that we *"feel"* offended! What, in us, needs the world to behave just the way, we, such a "perfect" being, demand? Why do we feel victimized? Oh, poor us. Or so we think.

We need some love and we need it now! So catch yourself, hopefully before full outrage takes hold, and laugh at your "poor little me" attitude and send it love. In fact, and this is big, send love to the *feeling* of rage. Send softness and kindness to your victim mentality.

Check yourself out whenever this little baby demands the world to be its way. Send this pitiful emotional crybaby the love it needs. There are too many little petty things that we permit to take us over and that limit our joy in the moment. Maybe so many of our needs were not met as children that we now, as adults, try to bully our way through the world, thinking every little thing has to go our way. A little too deep to go into for this book but, think on this: We may just be making up a drama about things and are allowing them to re-victimize us. We need to send love to the great playwright in us.

Please know that I am talking about things like waiting in line because somebody is filling out a check, traffic jams, somebody forgetting your birthday, the steak not being done perfectly, or not getting the emotional response you thought you should. These daily irritations turn us into Tennessee Williams, and make us write a backstory of self-delusion, anxiety and anger. These are the kinds of trivial things that we allow to hurt us. (To be clear: I am not talking about true abuse or real danger!) Pay attention to *your dramatic* self and send yourself the love you need.

Irritated? Send that irritation love. Disappointed? Send that disappointment love. Angry? Send that anger love. Send your negative emotion some love, as if it was something other than you – *because it is!* You are not that emotional state! (And that *is* a topic for another book.)

Joyful Love Tip #4:

Send love to your reactionary emotions. Think of the emotion as being the center of a target, right in the middle of the bull's-eye, name what you are feeling and simply send it loving thoughts. The reason you are reacting is not important. So do not add a story. In fact, another person in the same situation might not be bothered at all! Remember, you are *not* that fleeting emotion. Just think about how many emotions you go through in a day. Whew, the mind boggles! When I am upset I "try" to think about how fast this upset would pass if Johnny Depp walked in. (Sorry, guys... what if Beyoncé walked in?) My emotional state would flip in a second! We can choose our present state by sending love to our "victim thinking" in the moment. Humor helps too. You can devise your own "go to" pleasant thought to use. (Johnny works for me, and yes, my husband knows that I have a thing for Mr. Depp.)

LISTEN:

Who are you screaming at in your head? How long are you going to continue to tell that driver off, in your head? How many times will you have that same conversation with that so-and-so at work, in your head? When you hear yourself ranting, send that rant some love, send that disgruntled person some love, too. (Yes, that disgruntled person is you, yet again.)

Playful Practice: Target Love

Reflect on your emotional habits. Who or what constantly pushes your buttons? List just the main ones first. By writing them down, you will diffuse some of the energy around them. More than that, you will be prepared to send love to your emotions and the situations. Play Cupid for yourself by aiming for those emotions with arrows of love the moment they arise.

IMAGINE:

What if road rage around the world were gone? What if people stopped getting upset over not having their minor preferences always catered to? (Imagine this just for yourself! Wow, how peaceful your brain would be) Imagine all brains calm and loving themselves and their emotions Think of them all playing Cupid and hitting the target of their negative emotions with love. Just for fun, send love right now to all the brains in the world. Go ahead, try it. Emanate love from your brain to all brains. I just did. Picture a huge, never-ending sea of humans…connect with them all mentally and send all the positive loving energy you can!

Chapter Five: Weather Love

Everybody talks about the weather. It seems to be *the* opening sentence of choice, at least in the U.S. (If you are in another country and culture, please change the word "weather" to the most-used opening topic of conversation where you are.)

Even though we are looking at everything with love, sometimes narrowing the topic down really helps our focus for the moment. So, let's send love to the weather. Why? The sky and weather patterns touch the whole globe, so if we are aware of the weather at any moment during the day, we can send it our love and tag on love for all whom it affects. My dear mother always had me look up to the sky. "Look up, dear," she would say. So I was honored with having this habit of appreciating the beauty of the sky at any given moment. You can too! Simply send love to the beauty of the sky. It is never ugly. We are always caught by the majesty of the clouds; even on a totally grey day there is a gentle softness to them. Look, really look at the different colors of grey you see. Surely it is majestic, and the awe of it can overwhelm you. Use this joyful moment to send love to all of it and to all beings under it, and the planet too.

Think of the sky as your "love distribution mechanism." We are all connected by this one, ever-changing sky. You can use it as a connection to all things, too. The sky is really just like us, ever-changing, clouds coming and going like our thoughts, beautiful and sometimes uneasy and ready to storm. Yet, we give the sky more appreciation than we give ourselves. Are *you* not more beautifully complex and worthy of love? So, whenever you notice the sky, day or night, allow it to also remind you that *you* deserve love as well. As you send love to all whom the sky covers, include the beauty that is you. You are at least as important as the clouds. If you have to start appreciating yourself a little more, start there.

The weather and sky can be there for you in any moment you choose to use them as another tool for love. Maybe the breeze can also be a love vehicle for you? Remember, the night sky filled with stars works great too. We are "star-stuff," after all.

Joyful Love Tip #5

"Look up, dear." Use the weather and sky as a reminder to send love. Send love to the person you are talking to, this would be you, by the way, and mentally thank yourself for being a reminder as well. (I hope you are seeing a pattern here, to include yourself in all the love you ever send). See and appreciate the majesty of nature and send love to all who are under the sky. Then send love to all of nature.

LISTEN:

Listen to your inner dialogue about the weather and your outer banter. Use the ever-changing weather as a metaphor for non-attachment. You change constantly; in fact everything does. The only thing we can be sure of is change. It is all good. Enjoy the ride and send yourself love as you contemplate *your* majesty within nature.

Playful Practice: Weather Love

Look at your day. Do you check the weather? Do you prepare for it, such as deciding how to dress for the day? Pick a few "weather"-related habits or activities that can be a reminder to use the weather to send love to all. Maybe it's opening the blinds or adjusting the thermostat before you leave for the day. Make a list of a few such actions that can remind you to use the weather as another love generator.

IMAGINE:

What if everybody appreciated the beauty of the sky and the scope of the effect of weather and the beauty of nature? Imagine if all humans saw themselves as part of the glory of the sky? Think of all beings on the planet loving the beauty of "just looking up."

Chapter Six: "P.A.P." Love (Particularly Annoying People Love)

"I love because my love is not dependent on the object of love. My love is dependent on my state of being. So, whether the other person changes, becomes different, friend turns into foe, does not matter, because my love was never dependent on another person. My love is my state of being. I simply love."

Do As One

http://www.doasone.com/

This one is close to Target Love, but hits a bit closer to home. It is also a hard one, I admit. But, and this is a big but, when you accomplish this one, your life will really be more joyous. First, you have to understand two very basic premises:

First: Everything and everybody who crosses your path helps you grow.

Second: What bugs you in others is simply a reflection of what requires inner growth on your own part. These annoyances can become a reminder to go within and find out *why* they really bug you. What is it that *really* drives you crazy about them? Use these annoying people as a loving opportunity for some real self-growth.

For example, my older brother and I have totally opposite political views. I used to get crazy because I could not believe *he* was so hateful. Then I hit Facebook and I would get so mad about the political posts of others. I was being driven crazy by those people, or so I thought. In fact, after much reflection and heart-pounding rants, I realized that my brother, and all of the other "disagreeable people," were simply a reflection of my mean-spirited reactionary self. Yipers! Talk about a humbling experience. I felt like a child who is being punished for something she *did* do. I did not like the feeling, but I knew deep down that I deserved it. Now, when my brother goes off on some political rant, I am totally calm and simply say, "I am glad we live in America, no matter who is in office." Or I send him love and grant him the freedom to be who he has to be. I also send love to my "mean-spirited" self that wants to lash out and knock him on the side of the head. Of course, since fair means fair for both sides, I am sure he would like to knock me on the side of the head, too.

All annoyances need your love, self-love, to be more precise. Ideally, you need quiet time to allow for some introspection and reflection to discover more about your wonderful self. However, depending on when the "annoyance" happens, or the annoying person is in your face, this inner exploration is not always possible. So you can simply, upon noticing that agitation arising, send love to that person and to yourself right away. You see that their issues are their issues and they also need love; however, that negative inner feeling is *all*, I repeat *all*, about you. Yes, *you*!

Here's another example. There is a person annoying you, but if Mother Teresa were in the same situation, would she be annoyed? Probably not! Or suppose another person were married to your spouse? Would the same things annoy them? Heck, would your partner even be the same person they are? No! So you see, whatever dance you do with another person, place or thing, it is all about you! *You* are the common partner and the common denominator, you are the constant energy reacting from your personal point of view, or your private story to whatever is happening, no matter what! Some people hate to stand in line, for example, and start silently screaming at the slowpoke holding up the line. Perhaps this does not bother you at all, but we all know people who just cannot wait in line. Same situation but different "reactions." Remember: You bring yourself with you wherever you go!

When you begin to try practicing P.A.P. Love or "Particularly Annoying People Love," you will see how you are in control of reacting or responding to anything in your life. Is this easy? No! But it is so well worth it! By practicing this one little act of love you will find so much more peace, and by turning negative reactions into an opportunity to send love to another person, well, will be life altering.

Here is another example, especially for wives or mothers Do these things bug you or not? Socks under the bed? Wet towel on the quilt? Toilet seat up? Dirty clothes missing the hamper? No one else replacing the empty toilet paper roll? Fill in the blank with your own pet peeves. I actually do not mind any of the above. Really, I do not. I am not telling you this to blow my own horn but to let you know how "Annoyance Love" pays off. I leaned to send love to myself and to my darling husband over the years when these things happened. In fact, as I attend to all of the above "annoyances," I find I *adore* taking care of them. You see, I count them as proof I have him in my life, and boy, would I miss not having him there. Note that I am not "Little Miss Perfect," either. Learning this love practice was an effort for sure, but now my "chores" are not "chores" because I have chosen to see them as acts of love done with awareness and appreciation,

Now the harder part of practicing P.A.P. Love are all of those generally annoying people out there. All those people who suck! LOL! I know, right? You know who I mean, all those "idiots" out there, the hypochondriac relatives, the ignorant lowlifes, the bad drivers, the gullible jerks who end up costing us money, the "radicals," the bad guys, and the "others" who are not "us." It's okay to think of these others this way, after all they really *do* suck? Right?

Wrong! They all reflect traits someplace in us! And, get this, we are the people who "suck" to them! If we think other people suck, remember that *we* are part of "those" other people to them! So, guess what? We suck too!

That is why we do all we can to pay attention to those moments when "those" people annoy us. We need to love ourselves and learn the "why" behind our annoyed reactions.

To me, it is the fear that I could be like "them" that gets me. Then anger rises because I think *they* should be better. Of course, really it is my disappointment in myself and my feeling that I should be better. I do not want to dwell on negativity and get into psychoanalysis here. So, simply acknowledge that you are the same as the annoying "others" on some level and send yourself love, then send love to them.

The truth is, we are all just learning and doing the best we can with what we have. I am in first grade on some levels and a PhD on others. *So are you!* So are all of us. Judging others is really self-judgment, and we can be so cruel, so very cruel. So let's stop the madness, one annoyance at a time. It can start with that toilet paper roll, and remember that you have the power and capacity to expand it to everything and everybody!

Know we are all just part of a human family; we are all basically the same, just at different levels of thought and development. We all cross each other's paths for a reason and it is all for self-growth. Do you have an annoying spouse, sister, co-worker or neighbor? Use that person to nourish your loving work toward your own self-growth. Let that person be the catalyst to ignite your expanding love. If we can make the little things less annoying by awareness and love, then our drop in the ocean will multiply.

Turn commonplace annoyances into opportunities for self-love and to share love with the other person. If somebody else were in your situation, they would respond differently. It is all about *you* and *your* response. Use annoying things to improve your "skill set of love for yourself and others." You will find a much more peaceful life!

Joyful Love Tip #6: P.A.P. Love

Send love to the person annoying you *and* to yourself, the true origin of this feeling of annoyance. Send love to what it is in you that is causing this disturbance. Even if you do not know exactly what it is, send love!

LISTEN: What thoughts slam through your head when you get bothered…victim thinking? Snobby thinking? (Why can't they see what I see?) Royal thinking? (How dare they?) When emotion is high, rational thinking is low. So listen to the thoughts that trigger your anger. Send them love and then, when you can, figure out what is really being reflected back to you. Grow in love, in love with yourself, the situation and if a human is involved, with that person. Ask what *you* brought to the situation, and what you learned.

Playful Practice: P.A.P. Love

You may not need to line up a practice for this one, since Particularly Annoying People pop up everyplace! (And they will continue to do so until we master self-love.) However, we all have the P.A.P. we know we will be seeing. Sending love to yourself and to them *before* you encounter them can work miracles. So review in your mind the list of people you need the most help with. Set aside a moment before you encounter them to send loving thoughts to you both, picturing a more loving encounter.

Imagine: Take a moment to think about all the annoying people. Send "them" love, the ones who are *not* as "wonderful" and right-thinking as you. It sounds funny, doesn't it, since the "they" out there are just like you in between their ears, and *you* are their "they." Imagine if all of "them" took time to send love to their "annoying people" list. (Remember we could be on the receiving end when they do.) What a joyful place the world would be! Send that love every time you are annoyed by "them" and remember to send love to yourself!

Loving Reminders Page:

Joyful Love Tip #4: Target Love

Aim love at your current emotional state. Hit that targeted feeling with all of your love and grant yourself permission to ease into a new and more loving mental state.

Joyful Love Tip #5: Weather Love

Use the sky, wind, or even rain as a love delivery system to all. Remember, *you* are part of this exercise, too.

Joyful Love Tip #6: P.A.P. Love

Send love to the person annoying you *and* to yourself, the true origin of this feeling of annoyance. Send love to what it is in you that is causing this disturbance. Even if you do not know exactly what it is, send love!

Chapter Seven: Walking Love

Experienced meditators know there is slow walking meditation and fast walking meditation. I suggest that we lighten up the meditation part and simply send love to the earth with each step we take. You can vary this to fit wherever you are walking. If you are in a building, for example, send that love to the building as you walk. Science has proven that everything vibrates and that thoughts can change the direction of atoms. Even the molecular structure of water changes with positive thoughts and plants even grow better when they are given love. In fact plants actually physically react when a match is brought close to them too! So your intention and thoughts of sending love have validity. One of my favorite books about vibration and how we have the power to change the world with intention is *The Intention Experiment* by Lynne McTaggart.

With every step, you can mentally plant a lotus blossom! Use your walking to share love with the surface you are walking on. The earth is an obvious target, but our homes, workplaces and public spaces are vibrational entities, too. Ever notice the difference you see in an abandoned structure compared to an occupied one? The abandoned building looks "dead". So, as you walk anywhere, think of each footprint you leave as a love note. (If you jog, you can also think this way, and you will fly through the workout!)

Joyful Love Tip #7:

Every step can be an imprint of love for the earth, for yourself, and for those who follow you. We ambulate constantly. Even if you are on a walk to the bathroom you can leave loving footprints. (While you are there, remember to look into the mirror and send yourself a deep, loving message.)

THINK: With each step you take, have an awareness of gentleness, care, and loving energy projecting into your surroundings. Each step can also be a step of gratitude. (I'll have more to say about this in another chapter.) Walk with awareness, Try not to step on any living creature. Appreciate the skill and time it took to build the structure if you are indoors. Think of how your home protects and supports you. Walk with love and thanks in every step.

Playful Practice: Walking Love

Ask yourself how you can remember to use your steps as a loving gesture. Just going to and from your car can become your walking love. Look at your day and see your walking patterns as journeys of love.

IMAGINE: If you see others walking, imagine how their steps could also be filled with love. What if all humans walked with loving steps? How would the world be different if more of us were walking in love?

Chapter Eight: Action Love

So far, we have sent love through our eyes, touch, to all things and people, and through social media as well as when we walk but now we will focus on the very actions we are performing. It is a bit deeper so, the best way to explain this is through examples. There are actually a few parts to "action love." I guess you could call this "multi-tasking love" too.

Say you are ironing a shirt for your partner. Send love with every touch of the fabric while sending love to them. Now while you are adding love to the shirt, picture this love staying with your partner all day while he or she is wearing the shirt. As you iron, see your partner at work or wherever they will be, thereby "blessing" their day. (I know, I used that word again, but it is sort of a loving blessing.)

You can do this with anything, the dishes for example. Send love into the physical item, to your dishwasher, and then to the people who will use the dishes while they eat. Trust me, this takes the mundane to a new level. Sorting laundry, folding it and putting it away takes on a new feeling. Washing the car would become amazing! (I haven't done it, but suggesting it may just make me wash the car! Personally, I believe that is why God invented rain, but that is yet another book!) As I was writing this book, my clothes dryer buzzed, so I actually got to practice "action love."

Here are a few more examples:

Grocery shopping: When putting items into the shopping cart, send love to the food and then see the actual eating of it through love.

Dusting: This was not a favorite activity of mine, but it can be "almost" fun if you think of the action as loving your furniture and seeing those who use it with love.

Cooking: The best one! As you prepare it, infuse the food with your loving energy and see those who will be eating it with love! Remember to add yourself into all of this as well! See yourself in your love light!

At work: It's possible to transform tedious routines into uplifting and helpful rituals with a higher purpose. Send love to the person whose name is on the paper you have to file or send love to that employee as he enters your office, for what seems like the millionth time, asking for help. Each sweep of the broom or wipe of the towel can be filled with love to all those you are cleaning up after. No matter what you do, it can become an act of loving action.

Self-care: Here is an example that combines action love *and* self-love. Any time you are in the act of grooming or bathing, do it with great love! It can become a sweet ritual, especially since we do it daily and usually at the same time. Simply and attentively, have your inner self adore your outer self with awareness and awe. We are amazing creatures, no matter what we look like, or the state of our health or social status. Just being alive is a miracle, so love your preparation time and love yourself.

Joyful Love Tip #8:

Every action of service or duty can be infused with your love. Simply send loving thoughts to all the people on the receiving end of whatever you are doing (like writing a book, for example!).

LISTEN: While you practice Action Love, listen to your thoughts as they become sweet happy wishes for you and the ones you are serving with your actions. Pay attention and you will see, that as time goes by and this becomes a habit. Your thoughts will eventually change about all of those mundane tasks that were once annoying and almost painful duties. Adding the expanded loving thoughts to those you are helping changes your currently boring tasks into an expanding gift of love.

Playful Practice: Action Love

Pick three actions that you know you will perform today. These should be routine things that you usually do without thinking. Habitual actions are great for this and if you do not enjoy them, all the better. You may want to write them down as a reminder because they could be that "automatic." Then bring love and awareness to the action itself, to the other people benefiting from it, and to you, the performer, as you do them. Yes, simply brushing your teeth works because it means less bad breath for others to tolerate. Making coffee? Great! We know this really helps others! Opening the store or diner? Simply think of all those you will serve. You choose. You may really have to think about it. I know, sometimes we assume not thinking about things appears to make the mundane or annoying routines better, but in truth, infusing them with love will be transformational. I now *love* ironing; it is a morning ritual that I look forward to! Start with your three routines. Then you can expand to more actions anytime you think about it.

IMAGINE: What if all the people in the world performed their actions filled with their love? What if we all projected our love outward to those we served? What if everything were made with love, sold with love, bought and used with love? It is very possible, with simple but loving attention, starting with us. It's kind of cool to think about! See it, feel it…imagine the feeling if all was done with attentive, active love!

Chapter Nine: Gratitude Love

Now this gets really easy and hugely transformational! Andy Grant said in his course in gratitude that he likes to define it as "great attitude." If you are into any level of self- improvement, I am sure that you are aware of the power of gratitude. It makes sense to me that if you are not grateful for what you *do* have now, how could you be grateful for the *more* that you want? So let us get busy with gratitude love. Sending love to the good things and happenings in your life is fundamental. Silent thanks for green lights, synchronicities, surprise discounts, etc. are easy to start with. You are probably already doing this on some level. Of course, verbal thank-yous are just polite. I want to add a "do not take things for granted" thank you list here. It is important to say thank you for the mundane, habitual things others do for you. Think "thank you" for the tasks that automatically are done for us by unseen people, too.

"If the only prayer you ever say is thank you, it will be enough."

Meister Eckhart

Verbal Gratitude: If your mate is the trash "taker outer" in your house, say thanks. Notice the children when they do things as part of their day, including their homework. Give a thanks to a co-worker who always brings the reports, or emails them. Sure, it will give them a boost, but hold on here. It will also prove to you there are wonderful things going on *for you*!

Non-Verbal Gratitude: Now, add to the thank you list those personal helpers in our daily lives who are unseen "servants." Send a mental thanks to the people who pick up the trash or the recycling, the people who service our transportation systems or clean the streets. Do you see where I am going with this? Heck, the mail carriers sure need a loving thought of gratitude. Take a moment now, even if it is the only time you do it, and mentally think of as many "silent partners" as you can who make living better for you. Send them loving gratitude. If you feel up to it, you can write a list of as many people as you can think of. Maybe have your family participate, the awareness this will lead to could surprise you. It will open your heart to see how we are all connected. You will see that everyone, and in fact, everything leads you to this very moment. (Even reading this little book is connected to everything that has gone before it, both in your life and mine!) The list, by the way, would be impossible to end. One can aim to be in a delightful state of boundless gratitude.

There is one most wonderful person you must include on your thank you list. I know I said there are no "have to do's," but I am going to be a bit mean here, wink, wink. Send loving gratitude to yourself! Yes, right now, a few seconds of loving gratitude for *your* energetic contributions, known and unknown, you have made for others. Be grateful for the person you give to the world every day. Reading this book counts as showing how you care and are actively choosing to be more loving! You are pretty amazing, right?

Thank you, thank you, thank you,
_____. (Please read those "thank yous" again and be sure to add your name)

Joyful Love Tip #9:

Gratitude Love is a little different in a way. It's not just acknowledgement with thanks, but a deeper knowing that humans, with lives and feelings and joys and sorrows, are making our life happen around us. There's a connectedness that can happen when you *really* thank the clerk or send love to the trash person who will be picking up your refuse. Give everyone who serves you sincere thanks with a loving thought.

THINK: As you send loving thanks, know how lucky you are to have all of this help in your universe to make your life easier, safer, cleaner, and more livable. This happens because of other fellow humans out there servicing, inventing, and performing tasks to keep your world running. Pay attention to your loving thoughts and feelings as you send this love. It is okay to feel good, really, it is.

Playful Practice Love: Gratitude Love

This may be the practice that is the most obvious and logical of all on some levels. We have all heard the phrase "count your blessings." We all can look around and be grateful for "things" and relationships. All great coaches, saints and masters suggest having a gratitude practice or journal and writing down five things you are grateful for in the morning and then again at night. Please do this if you are so inclined, it rocks! But I want you to offer an audible "thank you" whenever possible and perform a silent sending of loving gratitude to the "others" in your world who help create the day for you. Express your gratitude for the unseen many who serve us all throughout the day. That computer you are reading from did not just appear from nowhere. (Well, it really did initially come from a thought but, again, that is another book.) Look around the room and send some love to all of those who made what you see possible! Create some sort of a reminder, anything will do, to prompt yourself to thank the people who brought you your day.

IMAGINE: How delightful your life is because of these other humans! Imagine if everyone recognized and thanked others, either out loud or silently, for their contributions! Remember to thank yourself! Send love to all, and that includes you, dear wonderful human that you are. There is a great course on gratitude by Andy Grant at Udemy.com (**https://www.udemy.com/the-power-of-gratitude/#/**).

Loving Reminders Page:

Joyful Love Tip #7: Walking Love

Every step can become a loving trace of your love on earth. Simply intend it to be so.

Joyful Love Tip #8: Action Love

Add loving thoughts to the physical actions you perform by sending loving thoughts to those you are affecting with your task. It's a way of paying it forward and backward.

Joyful Love Tip #9: Grateful Love

This is simply adding a loving thought about the magnificent human being you are and either verbally thanking or silently thanking yourself and others. It is a kind of humanization of the gratitude for services provided, and an additional loving connection coming from your heart to all of the people we depend on for a better life.

Chapter Ten: Food Love

Food Love is a yummy kind of love! This may be an interesting love tip to try. It has nothing to do with weight, nutrition, or being a vegetarian or a meat eater. It has everything to do with simply having a loving attitude toward food. In previous chapters we have already sent love to "everything" we see, smell and touch, but I feel that food deserves its own chapter. That's because it is so important to us and there seems to be a war against food going on. Every day we are told another food is bad for us or that we should be eating more of yet another food. Watch your calories, watch the sugar, and watch the fat. Yipers! It can drive a person crazy.

Instead, what about loving the foods you *do* eat? What if you were really sending love to each bite and sip? How about sending love to all of the people who got the food to you, and sending some love to all of the elements that had to come together to produce the food (the sun, rain, and earth)? Really love the very fact you *can* eat and have something to eat. How lucky! Even if you are eating gluten-free cardboard smeared with water, really *love* it. Eating should always be a pleasure, and no matter what choices you make, do so with love. If you think about it, feeding yourself is an act of self-love. It's a pretty cool way to think about something as necessary and automatic as eating. But, if we did not do this simple act, or could not do it, along the way we would not be happy campers and we would die.

So, no matter what you pick up and put into your mouth, do so with love. Love for the very process of converting the food to energy, the taste, the texture and the fragrance. The process of digestion is an incredible feat the body performs, so love your body for all that happens during the entire act of eating. If you do not know much about the function of digestion, learn more, because it will amaze you. Lovingly consume each meal and snack. You have time as you chew to appreciate all that goes into the magic of eating.

Joyful Love Tip #10

Send love to yourself while you eat, to the food you are eating, to the forces it took to get it to you and to the incredible body you have that will convert it all so you can stay alive. You may want to look up Dr. Emoto and his experiments with sending different emotions to water. It is fascinating research indeed. He shows how the crystals of water change and are significantly altered when negative words are said or are simply taped to the beaker, as opposed to when positive words are used.

Visit here for more information: http://www.masaru-emoto.net/english/hado.html.

Playful Practice: Food Love

This practice is wide open for you. Many of us are fortunate that food is abundant for us, and eating is one of the great joys of life. How you remind yourself to remember this is up to you and depends on your lifestyle. A note on the fridge is a good idea, but after a while you will no longer "see" this reminder unless you move it somewhere less expected, like the silverware drawer. If you love to dine out, a reminder note in your wallet may help you to remember this practice. A picture of a heart on the inside of your cabinets may do the trick, too. Take a moment to list three places or times in the day that you may need a reminder to send that love to yourself and your food as you eat. Maybe surrounding yourself and the food with love could even help you eat more consciously and wisely? Not a bad side effect.

LISTEN: While you are eating, listen to what you are thinking. Are you hating yourself for the indulgence, are you angry while you eat? Is that bully voice taking over? Are you just in a "no joy" mode? If so, simply become aware while you taste the food and become joyful for the sheer pleasure of eating. This will remind you to send love to entire eating process. By just listening to your thoughts you can bring loving awareness and gratitude for what you are doing and to those who brought this food to you.

IMAGINE: How wonderful it would be if we all took real joy in eating! Picture the world well-fed and everyone enjoying their food with poise, grace and ease, sending love to each morsel and savoring the effort that brought them their meals.

Just for fun: Visit this web site: www.loveshaker.com.

You can "Shake" love all over your food…or anything for that matter!

Chapter Eleven: Time Travel Love – Past and Future

Past Time Love

This one may hit you a little sideways. But modern science is beginning to see that time does not exist and that is a construct of man's (think Albert Einstein and the Law of Relativity). Time ends up being an illusion, if you will. Quantum physics experiments show that thoughts *can* be passed from one person to another and that they can change our reality. A great book to read is E^3 by Pam Grout. We have all experienced moments of déjà vu, or have thought of somebody and then they called us out of the blue after we hadn't heard from them for years. Our own life experience is filled with unexplainable mental connections (if we pay attention). I propose that you send loving thoughts to your past. If you are brave enough, even send them to your painful past. If that is not comfortable, no worries.

Your current memories and reactions in the present are all based on how you perceive your past experiences. Your past leaves traces of these memories in you, some pleasant and some not so pleasant. So why not love ALL of you just a little more? We all deeply believe our past stories, yet, if you and I were at the same accident at the same moment, our "story" about it would be different because of our past frames of references that we each have lived. The *who* you are is who you bring to everything and this *who* is based on all of our past experiences, Sending love to our past therefore sends love to our own present being,

I'll share my own experiences here: I did an exercise in which I sent love to myself as a preemie in the hospital. When I was born prematurely, I had to stay in the hospital for a month. In those days, hospital staff did not touch preemies. Back then no one knew how important being held was to an infant. The "failure to thrive" theory was unknown and perhaps they were more afraid of infection. (It was 1951 after all.) So I figured my abandonment issues may have stemmed from that. Oh my! Imagining myself as a three-pound, seven-ounce baby alone for a month was a tearful experience! I imagined holding my tiny self and giving little Denise the love and cuddling she needed. I still can get emotional thinking of how that baby must have felt. Sending love to images of yourself as a child can be very therapeutic. Again, if this is too difficult, simply skip this exercise. You may consider starting with the less painful times in your past that could use a little love. (Remember, you can use this little book any way you choose.)

As an alternative, you can think outside yourself, and send healing energy to the past of others or even to happenings in history. My hubby watches everything about World War II, and as you might imagine, this is not my cup of tea. No worries! I simply send love to all of those images and the people who were caught up in it all. Yes, I even send love to the "bad guys." All of that pain is still being felt, at least in our collective unconscious. We all know how this impacts our world every day. It all needs healing. I add myself in there as well because I am being exposed to the negativity.

So use sending love to the past any way that suits you. I do it when I get angry with something that happened long ago that I see I have not "really" gotten over. You know that pesky "baggage" that weighs us down. It truly helps. You can just send love to the situation first, then eventually you can get to the people and yourself. So this "Past History Love" can help *us* heal and help the world heal too. I kind of see this as a cooling ointment we can spread to soothe the old wounds, and kind of minimize scars and neutralize the negative. Sending love to right now to Danny Beckett, who turned me down when I asked him to the Sadie Hawkins dance! And to my wedding photographer, who did not take the right pictures and to…oh sorry…Boy, it's a good thing love multiplies the more we share!

Joyful Love Tip #11.1

Send love to your own past and to the historic past of the world. We spend plenty of time reliving our memories, so why not work at healing them? Be gentle and kind to yourself. Remember the negative and positive things all came together to get you right where you are now. Together they contributed to the wonder of you! Send love to the situation, and if possible to the people, and to yourself. Too hard? No worries, just work on history; it needs your love big-time.

LISTEN: What kind of thoughts were going through your head while reading about sending love to your past? We all have a past that needs loving. We can help it lose its power by sending it "brotherly" love. We cannot change it, but we can diminish the power it still has over us. Something is better than nothing, so when your mind goes to a not-so-pleasant thought from the past, send it a little love. Instead of staying there and conjuring up more unpleasantness, give it a blast of heart light and forgiveness.

IMAGINE: What if everybody could and would send loving thoughts to their past! It might put psychologists out of business! I wonder what sending healing thoughts to the past would release if we all did it? If you think about it, so many wars are really based on *past* anger and wrongdoings that happened in the ages ago. Our insecurities are too. Sending love to our personal history and to the history of the world and earth would be amazing. Imagine that new world with a past that was loved! After all, your past is all part of what got you to choose this book! All of your past brought you to these very words! Actually, if one action had been different in your past, you would not be reading these words. Kind of cool when you think about it.

Joyful Love Tip #11.2

Future Time Love

This is your cure for worrying. Most of the time, as we gaze into the future, we are shrouded in dread and fear. I propose we reverse this and really create a magical future for ourselves! We are nearing the end of this little book and I feel my "savior complex" kicking in, my dear reader. So I cannot let you go without this tip for a more loving and joyful future. Set yourself up for a great life by sending love to *all* of your future endeavors! Fill the "what" that you are imagining with love, light, energy and delight! If you do start to worry, send love to that as well (see Joyful Love Tip #4). Then picture your future happening with a shining light of love and joy. Worry serves no purpose. Planning and preparation do, but not worry.

Most of us expend so much energy "pre-living" in fear that we actually set the stage for failure. This little book has had you imagining in the most positive way, so please continue this going forward and assist others to do so as well. If you have a negative friend going on and on about a future filled with fear, you may ask, "What good do you think could happen?" Or, "Can you picture a better outcome?" At least help that person see that there is an alternative reality that he/she can imagine.

We so love drama that we invent it *before* it even happens! Do you have a job you dread? Try to ride to work in a bubble of love, fill your workplace with it, and imagine friendship and cooperation. See yourself working in ease and joy. Look for those good things as they happen during the day. As you send love to your future self and to your future in general, you are physically sending energy into the ether, the atomic structure that creates the future. If that theory is too far out for you, then you can just buy into my suggestion because thinking in a positive way can't hurt. Right?

LISTEN: What thoughts do you have while you envision future events? Are they fearful or happy? Smile at yourself and honor the idea that you may be a great novelist in the making, or perhaps a great prophet. No matter, marvel at the workings of your mind. It is all good and very human. Here is a huge tip: We may not be able to control how or when a thought pops into our mind, but we sure are responsible for how long it stays there!

Playful Practice: Time Travel Love (Past and Future)

This is a very internal practice, since living in the past and future is what we humans do most. Do you do better with positive or negative reinforcement? You may have to devise ways to "catch" yourself when you get into your mental time machine and find yourself caught in a story, or worse still, in that dreaded sleepless night re-living what happened during the day Personally, I say: "STOP" and make myself think about something else. At first I would stay stuck for hours in my merry-go-round of powerlessness and dread, but I now only stay there for a few moments. With a little practice you will be able to catch yourself earlier and earlier. Wearing a rubber band on your wrist and snapping it when you catch yourself "time traveling" may work for you. I just pay attention to the tension in my body. If my heart is pounding, or I "feel" tight, or I'm getting jittery or getting sickly in the stomach, that's always a clue I'm getting lost in time. My inner bully voice also gets louder.

So, this time travel thing will have to be an experiment for you. Look for triggers. For me, getting to work or coming home would trigger my negative "time travel." Getting up in the morning can throw you into both past and future time travel. So take a moment and think of your triggers and devise a way to help you catch yourself before you step into your mental time machine. Being in the present moment may surprise you! More and more joyful moments will fill your life, and in a way, this too is really sending love to yourself. (I highly suggest reading anything and everything by Eckhart Tolle for help with being present.) But the fastest way to get in the moment is to pay attention to your breathing. *All* of your attention. Take a moment and try it now. Go ahead, just breathe, you have nothing to do right now but to breathe.

IMAGINE: What a delightful world it would be if we all stopped putting fear and dread into the future! How uplifting it would be if we all send love to where we were going and to what we wanted to accomplish! Imagine what you want to do after reading today. Send sweet love and glowing light to your immediate future, even if it is sleep.

Chapter Twelve: Breathing Love

I saved this one until last, it's my personal favorite, and it is the easiest!

This is not my creation at all, as it is based on an ancient Buddhist practice called "tonglen."

"Tonglen means giving and receiving. You offer out love to the one who is caught in fear and pain and terror, and then you literally invite suffering into your heart to be transformed with love, and breathe it out. This is not an imaginary movement, you literally are moving energy. You literally are changing things. I know it may not feel like that at first, it may feel mechanical. But if you persist, you may start to feel how, when there is something violent on the news, instead of judgment the heart opens with compassion not only for the victims but the perpetrators of that violence." -- AARON   www.deepspringcenter.org

This is perfect because you have to breathe anyway, right? So you might as well make the most of it. At first I thought I had discovered this incredibly mind-blowing, life-altering act of love! Then of course, as with all great ideas, I realized that somebody else had already hit on it. It was the Buddha, actually. True, mine has my own little twist, but I have to admit that tonglen was my inspiration and it alone will change your life! Here is the "Denise" version.

Breathe in and think of something loving. It can be the beauty of nature, your feeling for your partner or child, or if you are so inclined, any deity or simply the energy of the universe. Choose the highest, most loving thought you can muster. Breathe it in deeply. Then as you exhale, you *add* your own love to it, thereby increasing all the love in the universe. Now, my twist is that you practice doing this everywhere you go. Add it to your practice of "Out and About Love," or when you're in traffic, during Thanksgiving dinner, sleeping next to your partner or child, at the beach… at any place and all the time! Your world will open up! As always, send some to yourself.

As Don Miguel Ruiz says:

"The whole world can love you, but that love will not make you happy.

What will make you happy is love coming out of you."

Joyful Love Tip #12

Breathing Love

Simply breathe in the highest thoughts/energy/love or goodness you can, and add your own to it as you exhale.

LISTEN: What choices go through your mind as you choose what to inhale? What choices go through your mind as you summon your highest thoughts to send out with each exhale? Listen to your thoughts to see if sending this love is more difficult to do to some people and easier to do to others. What is this judgment all about? Send love to your feelings of judgment, too.

Playful Practice: Breathing Love

Start this practice of breathing love during times of the day that you know you are calm, when you have moments to yourself. Even just three breaths will be perfect. So list a few times during the day that you are sure to have some peace. You see, breathing love during these times, rather than slipping into time traveling (as we discussed in Chapter 11), will give you an even deeper peace. Now, here's the challenge practice. What moments in the day are the worst? Remember, just take three deep breaths of inhaling and sending love, maybe 45 seconds each, during these most trying moments.

IMAGINE: What if all people everywhere were joining you in this breathing of love? What if all children were taught this simple idea? How would the world change? How fast would this change happen? Imagine all the people loving in this way! Imagine how you will feel, should you make this a habit. Remember, you can change the world around you, we all can!

Loving Reminder Page:

Joyful Love Tip #9: Food Love

Send love to the food, the processes, and the people who made the food possible and to yourself, the glorious body digesting it all.

Joyful Love Tip #11.1 and 11.2: Time Travel Love: Past and Future

Send love to the past that contributed to your journey so far and to your future experiences that will unfold the magic of your becoming.

Joyful Love Tip #12: Breathing Love

Breathe in all the positive, sacred, loving energy you can muster, add your own love and exhale this bountiful expansive divine additional love to the universe.

One last IMAGINE: Imagine the new loving life you are now part of and we are all one in this glorious love! Imagine if everyone did even just one of these love exercises. Imagine the new loving you, living in joyful harmony with yourself and others! I am just an ordinary person and it does indeed work, and is working for me. I am calmer, less judgmental, easier to live with, less moody, more aware and much, much more peaceful. It is nothing short of amazing. What a wonderful loving world we can all create, simply by adding more love. Person by person!

"Small acts, when multiplied by millions of people can transform the world!"

Terri Van Horn, Healinglightonline.com

CONGRATULATIONS!

Time to Celebrate!

"Why should I celebrate?" you ask. First, celebrate because you have just changed the world! Simply by reading and thinking about love, you have set more love in motion! So congratulate yourself and celebrate that! Remember that you and everybody else who reads this little book are making more love happen. The word "love" has been repeated in your mind many times and you have emanated love by doing some of the activities.

(I think Dr. Emoto would be very happy, since we are about 70% water, and we must have changed some of our molecular structure just by reading the word "love" so often! Over 450 times actually.)

All of this is delightful indeed. But there is a huge, very personal reason you should celebrate. Here's my own story: I learned about personal celebration from a most wonderful woman and nationally certified coach, Dana Phillips. (She is a Franklin Covey Personal Coach, a member of the Worldwide Association of Business Coaches, and holds credentials from the International Coach Federation. You can reach her at dana@teamconnections.org if you want to connect with her.)

I had finished a coaching course with Dana and she asked how I was going to "celebrate." There was silence on my end of the phone. You see, I had no idea that the concept of celebrating a personal win even existed. So in her kind way, she asked me again. I confessed to her that the thought of celebrating myself would never have crossed my mind. Well, from that moment on, my life changed in a very profound way! She explained how vital it is to positively reinforce our accomplishments and to acknowledge the things we have completed. It sends a most powerful message to the brain, both consciously and subconsciously. She told me that it is not a matter of huge or costly celebrations but a matter of *intent*. In other words, you can simply gift yourself a few moments on the deck with a cup of tea, or a hot bath, or a run…whatever gives you a feeling of joy! (I planned my celebration for writing this book as I typed this!)

I suggest that you even "celebrate" each time you remember to use one of the twelve joyful love tips in this book. You can do so by sending love to yourself, or actually give yourself a real pat on the back. The more often you reward yourself, the stronger your success factor will be. I am still working with this myself for dusting and using the vacuum. All I have to do is pre-decide what my celebration will be and then my house nearly cleans itself. I used this all during the writing of my book too. In fact, after the first draft was finished, I bought myself my first bouquet of flowers, ever!

Make a list of "celebrations" you can reward yourself with and keep it handy. Soon your life will be filled with intentional joyful moments and you will feel at ease. (For me, my house is actually cleaner! A miracle in itself!) And, and this is a *big* "and," it is a great way to move forward from being stuck. You see, you already have planned a tangible reward after you do the task at hand. So you have motivation to start the action you may be avoiding.

Since that call, I have thanked Dana every day of my life. I had a stressful job and I had a birthday card with the song "Celebrate" in it, and I played it so much I wore it out! If this hint for happiness is the only thing you gain from my little book, then I have paid it forward. (And maybe I have come up with the title of my next book, "Hints for Happiness.") Thank you, Dana, for making my world a better place and a better world for so many!

Here you go. Prepare to be amazed as your life unfolds with more ease and joy. Remember it is the *intent*, not the content of what you do. Putting on new polish counts, using cologne after you shave does too. Celebration is a simple and fun act of self-love. Imagine if everybody loved themselves a little more every day. Start your celebration list here and now. Grab a pen and paper and jot down a list of anything you can do with joy and self-love to celebrate and honor yourself for little and big successes.

You Take Over From Here

Since I want this little book to really work for you, it is now your turn to examine any areas that may specifically need your loving thoughts. You may choose to follow my outline or simply list needy areas that I may have not mentioned. You have extraordinary love to add to any place that may need a little more loving. Remember to lovingly put your joy first. You are whole, perfect and complete just the way you are. Sometimes we just forget that. The little voice that is thinking behind what you are reading *knows* this. Honor your goodness, because you are all goodness.

A Final Word

Using any part of this little book will ensure you will never be bored! You can look at anything at any time and in any place and send it love, whether you are eating, sleeping or cleaning. Love can become your constant inner mental activity. That is my deepest wish for you, a life of gentle and loving inner banter while you are adding more loving energy to the world. You can live a silent life of beautiful service for all. We are all the drops in the ocean and we are, by being love, making the ocean even more beautiful, one drop at a time. And in fact the ocean is only drops becoming one massive and powerful entity. Think of the power held in the ocean! You have it in you, my dear reader, to shift the world into complete love. You are both the drop and the ocean. Please share your loving additions on the group Facebook page **Just Add Some Love,** every drop matters.

A Little Something Extra

Prayer of St. Francis of Assisi

Lord make me an instrument of your peace,

Where there is hatred let me sow love;

Where there is injury pardon;

Where there is doubt faith;

Where there is despair, hope;

Where there is darkness, light;

And where there is sadness, joy.

O Divine Master,

Grant that I may not so much seek to be consoled as to console;

To be understood as to understand;

To be loved as to love;

For it is in giving that we receive;

It is in pardoning that we are pardoned;

And it is in dying that we are born to eternal life.

Invocation to Love

By: Renae' Mussachio

Channeled Invocation to Love
(please repeat 3x in a row if it resonates with you)

I allow love to live within me as I live within it.
I welcome love in every cell of my being.
I have love within my body and energy and now express it to my body, my energy and all that I am on all levels and through all dimensions.

I send love to all energy and release damage in all dimensions.
I send love to everyone and everything and release hatred.
I send love to the worlds, the universes and All That Is as anger is released from the consciousness and all else.

My consciousness is love.
My consciousness is light.
My consciousness is free.
I send my consciousness to the world and it expands for all to see, feel and know.

I am free.
I am free.
I am free to be me.

Thank you.
Thank you.
Thank you.

Love to all.
Love to all.
Love to all now. Thank you.

A Few Extra Thoughts

"All you need is love, all together now
All you need is love, everybody
All you need is love, love
Love is all you need."

John Lennon & Paul McCartney

"I fill myself with love and I send that out into the world. How others treat me is their path. How I react is mine."

Dr. Wayne Dyer

"To find the beloved you must become the beloved."

Rumi

And a video you might enjoy from Chris Cade (http://www.chriscade.com):

www.videosmotivational.com/best-clips/spirituality-videos/the-power-of-love/#video

Imagine

Keith Allen Kay

http://fractalenergymandala.com/

Imagine into the glory of Love
Imagine into the wish fulfilled
Imagine into the wonder of life
Imagine and you shall become
Within the Kingdom of Love are many dwelling places
States of experience created from Imagination
Fantasy has shown you the Doorway of Desire
Imagination opens that Door and enters into
You are Creation and Creator
You are Awakened Imagination
Forget the dream of suffering, separation and sin
You are from the Beginning
You are the Creative Word
You are the Kingdom of Love
You are Love's habitation
Cast off dreams and stories, old and tired
You are an Ever New story
Are you ready to turn the page?

About the Author

Denise Carey is a motivational speaker, a direct sales business coach, and a graduate of Marcia Wieder's Dream Coach University. She has studied metaphysics, positive thinking and all matters of spirituality since 1969. She is also a Light Body Graduate and has taken courses in Abundance, Reiki, Gratitude and Science of the Mind. Her degree is in Speech and Theater from Rowan University, Glassboro, NJ. She finally discovered her purpose in life after reaching her sixties, namely "to share joy, to live in joy and to help others to do the same." Denise currently lives in Haw River, NC, with her "most wonderful" husband, Christopher. Contact her at: joyandlove777@gmail.com and you can join the **Just Add Some Love** Facebook group for more encouraging and loving inspiration.
www.facebook.com/justaddsomelove

66689572R00043

Made in the USA
Columbia, SC
23 July 2019